PHYSICS FOR KIDS: ELECTRICITY AND MAGNETISM

PHYSICS 7TH GRADE
CHILDREN'S PHYSICS BOOKS

BABY PROFESSOR
EDUCATION KIDS

Speedy Publishing LLC

40 E. Main St. #1156

Newark, DE 19711

www.speedypublishing.com

Copyright 2017

In this book, we're going to talk about electricity and magnetism. So, let's get right to it!

INTRODUCTION TO ELECTRICITY

You use electricity in your home every day, but you may not know what electricity is. The computers, lamps, and air conditioners that you use are all powered by electricity.

SISTERS USING LAPTOP TOGETHER AT HOME

REAL LIGHTNING BOLT STRIKE IN A CITY

Outdoors, if there's a thunderstorm with lightning, then that's a form of electricity. You can't see it, but inside your body, there's a form of electricity as well. Without electrical signals your brain wouldn't work.

To understand some basics about electricity, you need to understand what an atom is and how the parts of an atom function together. Atoms can't be seen with your eyes, but all the matter in the universe is made up of them.

ATOM

RESEARCHER HOLDING A TRINITROTOLUENE
MOLECULAR MODEL

Atoms are so small that it takes billions of them to make up the everyday objects that we see. It's been estimated that the human body has this number of atoms--7 with 27 zeroes after it--7,000,000,000,000,000,000,000,000,000!

For a long time, scientists thought that the atom didn't have parts, but eventually it was discovered that it has three major components. These components are electrons, which have a negative charge, protons, which have a positive charge, and neutrons, which have no charge.

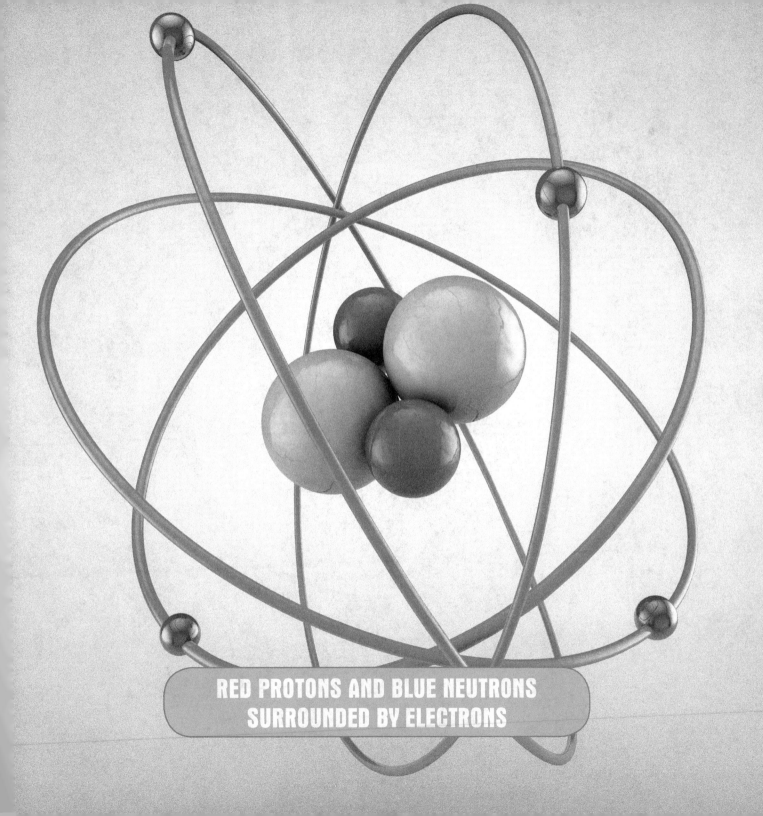

RED PROTONS AND BLUE NEUTRONS
SURROUNDED BY ELECTRONS

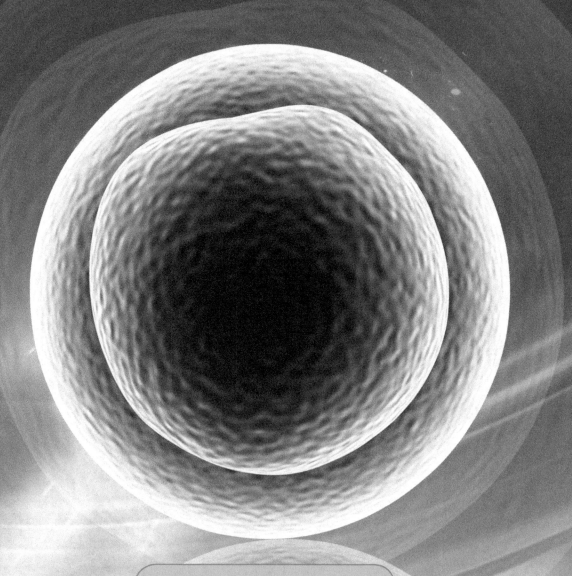

CELL WITH NUCLEUS

In the center of every atom is a nucleus. The protons and neutrons are located there, but the electrons travel around the nucleus and they spin quickly. In fact, if the protons with their positive charges weren't there, the electrons would just fly off the atoms. So, in summary:

Proton—a subatomic particle that holds a positive charge

Neutron—a subatomic particle that holds no charge

Electron—a subatomic particle that holds a negative charge, these form electricity

The amount of charge a proton carries and the amount of charge an electron carries are the same. The proton carries a positive charge and an electron carries a negative charge. The most stable atoms will have an equal number of each and they will balance each other out.

NUCLEAR CHAIN REACTION

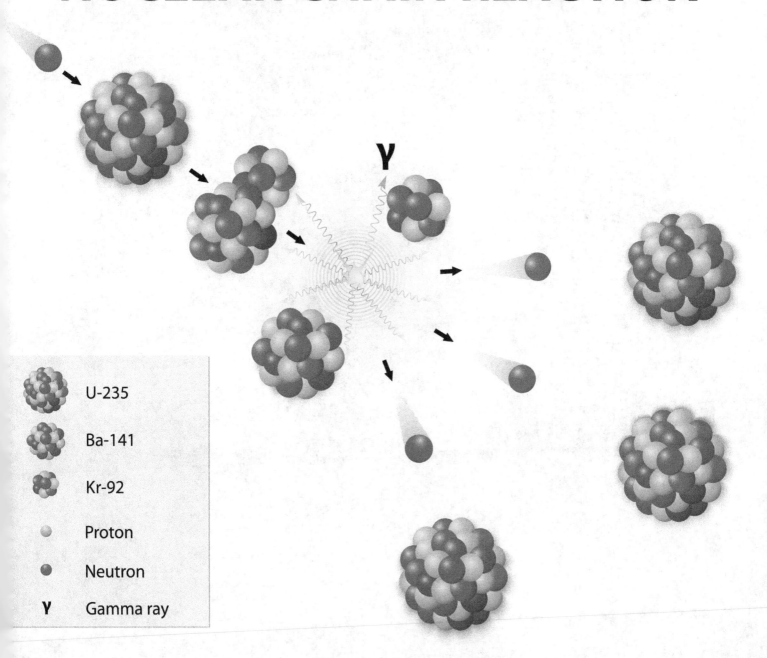

U-235

Ba-141

Kr-92

Proton

Neutron

γ Gamma ray

BLUE PROTONS AND NEUTRONS IN NUCLEUS
AND SURROUNDED BY A CLOUD OF ELECTRONS

Atoms of some substances are more stable than others. The electrons on the outer orbit of an atom don't always stay with their atoms. These electrons have a special name. They are called valence electrons.

WHAT IS ELECTROSTATIC FORCE?

There's a force that comes into play when particles of different charges get close to each other. They either repel each other or they attract each other. This force is called electrostatic force.

MOLECULE CUBIC CRYSTAL STRUCTURE

STATIC HAIR

An electron and a proton attract each other, because they have opposite charges. This is the force that keeps an atom together. Two electrons both have negative charges so they would repel each other or push away from each other. Two protons would both have positive charges, so they would repel each other as well.

FLOWING CHARGES

Imagine that we have a group of atoms that are packed tightly together. When we apply some force, either positive or negative, we can knock out an electron from one of the atoms. Then, that electron, which is floating free, moves to the next atom and tries to join it. In doing so, it pushes out another electron, which is now loose and moves to the next atom. This is a very simple explanation of how electrical current works.

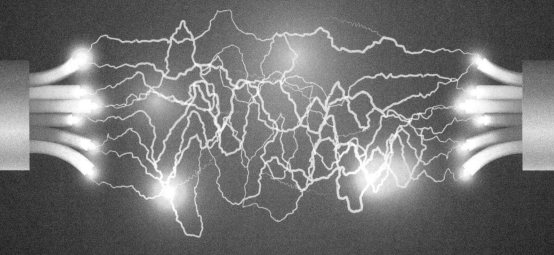

ELECTRIC LIGHTNING BETWEEN CABLES

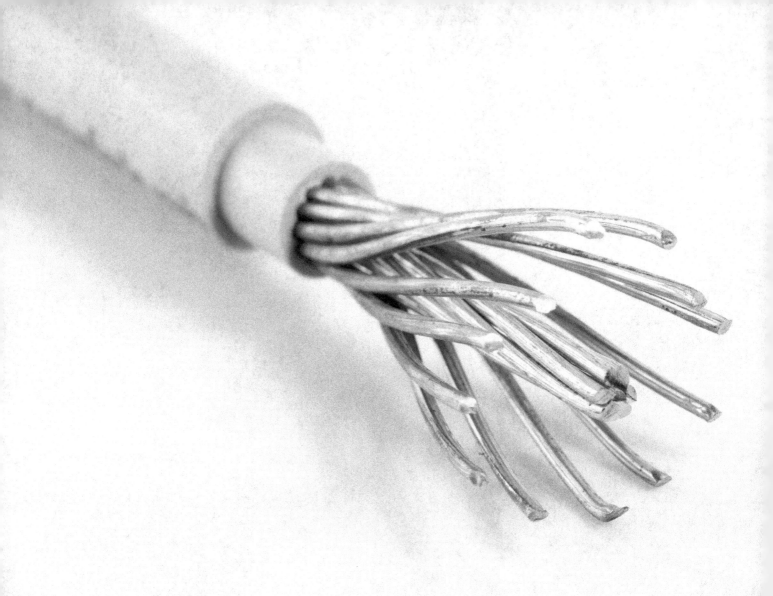

COPPER WIRE

Some elements are better conductors of electricity than others. To get good electrical current, you would use an element like copper that doesn't hold on to its valence electrons too tightly. Electricity is essentially a flow of electrons from one place to another.

INTRODUCTION TO MAGNETISM

Have you ever stuck a magnet on your refrigerator door? You can feel the force in your hand as the magnet gets closer and when you place it there, it sticks as if it had some type of invisible glue. The "glue" is an invisible attraction that you can't see, but it has to do with positive and negative charges.

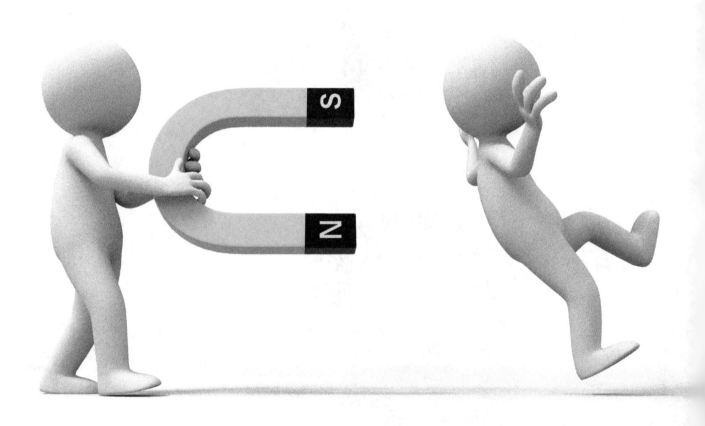

TWO MEN AND A MAGNET

The atoms in almost all objects have electrons that spin randomly in different directions. Magnets are unique. In a magnet, the molecules are organized so that all the electrons are spinning the same way. This creates an object that has two poles—a north pole and a south pole. The magnetic current flows from the north pole of the magnet to the south pole of the magnet and it creates an invisible field around the magnet.

If you put two magnets next to each other, the north pole of one will attract the south pole of the other and vice versa. If you put their north poles together, they will repel each other and the same is true of the south poles. If you put them together, they will repel each other. They work just like protons and electrons. You can't see the forces that make this happen, but they're still there!

BOY HOLDS TWO MAGNETS TOGETHER

MAGNET SEPARATING STEEL AT DEMOLITION SITE

WHICH MATERIALS MAKE GOOD MAGNETS?

Only certain elements will make good magnets. Iron is the element most frequently used. Because the manmade material steel has a lot of iron in it, it can act as a magnet as well.

THE EARTH IS A MAGNET

Just like a handheld magnet that's made of iron, the Earth's core is primarily made of iron. This means that Earth itself is a gigantic magnet! Its North Pole and South Pole are the poles of its magnetic field. This is the reason a compass needle points north so you can find your direction when traveling.

HAND HOLDING COMPASS

FLOCK OF MIGRATING CANADIAN GEESE

Many different types of birds and sea creatures can sense the magnetic field of the Earth as they make migrations of thousands of miles in the air or under the sea. The Earth's magnetic field acts as a "force field" protecting us from the sun's potentially damaging radiation and solar wind.

THE RELATIONSHIP BETWEEN ELECTRICITY AND MAGNETISM

Physicists, scientists who study physics, use the word "electromagnetism" to describe the force that attracts protons to electrons. They also use it to show how the flow of electrons causes electricity and the resulting magnetic field.

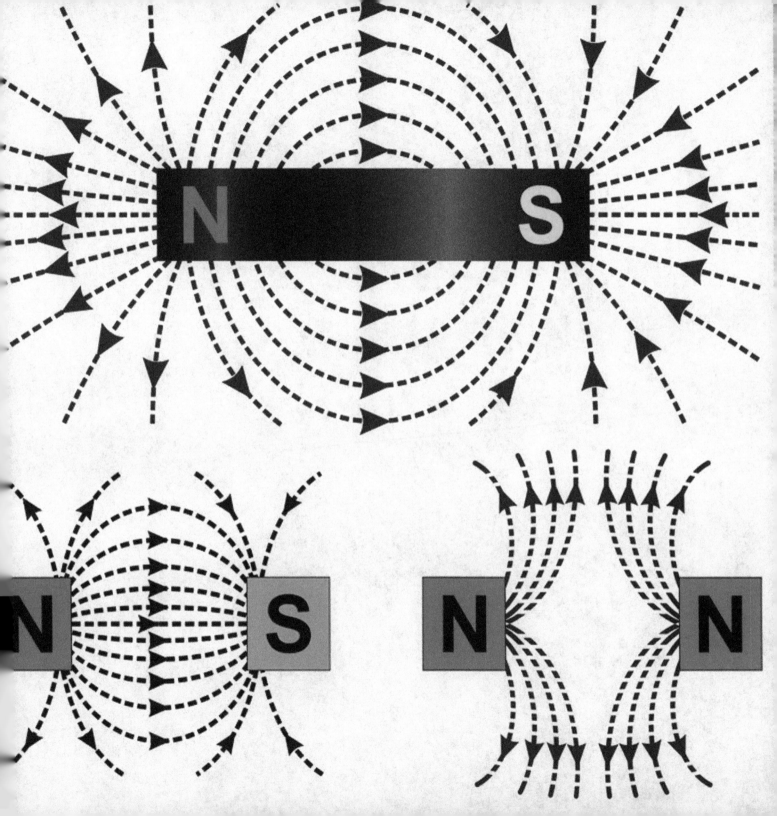

You can use electricity to create a strong magnet. A cylindrical iron bar with a copper wire wrapped around it can be used to create a powerful magnet. When electrical current is run through the copper wire, it creates what is known as an electromagnet.

When electricity begins to flow through a conductor, like a copper wire, it creates a magnetic field. This field can be increased further by making the wire more coiled. The more coiled the wire is, the more electrical current can move through a shorter distance. The coiling of the wire in a tighter space increases the power of the magnetic field.

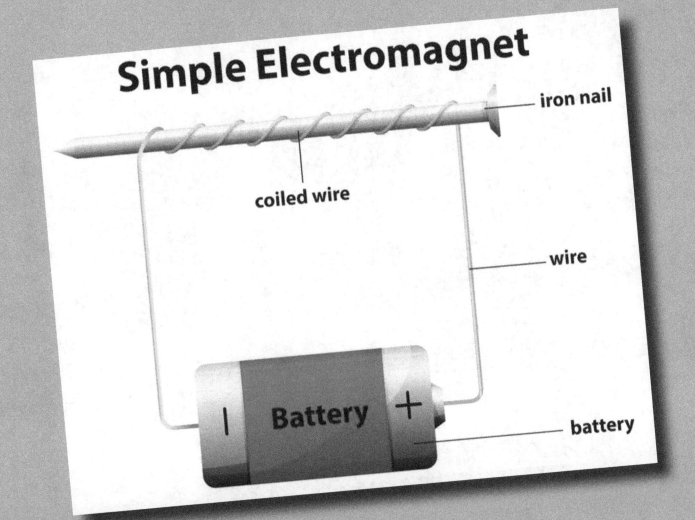

ILLUSTRATION OF THE SIMPLE ELECTROMAGNET

ELECTRIC MOTORS DRIVING INDUSTRIAL WATER PUMPS AT POWER PLANT

ELECTRIC MOTORS

Electromagnetism is very important since one of its applications is the creation of electrical motors. It's impossible to go through the day without being around electric motors. If you go through your house you will find them everywhere—the washing machine, the electric toothbrush, the hair dryer, the electric razor, and the vacuum cleaner are just a few of the common items in your house that have electric motors.

Electric motors use energy from electricity to create physical movement. For example, think about an electric beater. You plug it into the wall outlet and electricity goes through the wire to the motor, which turns those beater pieces so that you can whip up some egg whites and make a meringue for a pie.

MAN USING AN ELECTRIC EGG BEATER

WOMAN LOOKING AT COMPUTER PROCESSOR COOLER FAN

Your computer has electric motors too. It has one that turns a fan to keep the computer cool as it operates. It has another to make the hard drive run, and a third to open and shut the drive where you place CDs in order to read them.

ELECTROMAGNETIC INDUCTION

We can use electricity and transform it by using electric motors to create the movement we need to make appliances run. There's another important way that electromagnetism can be used as well. Instead of using electrical current to make movement, it uses movement to create electrical current. This process is called induction.

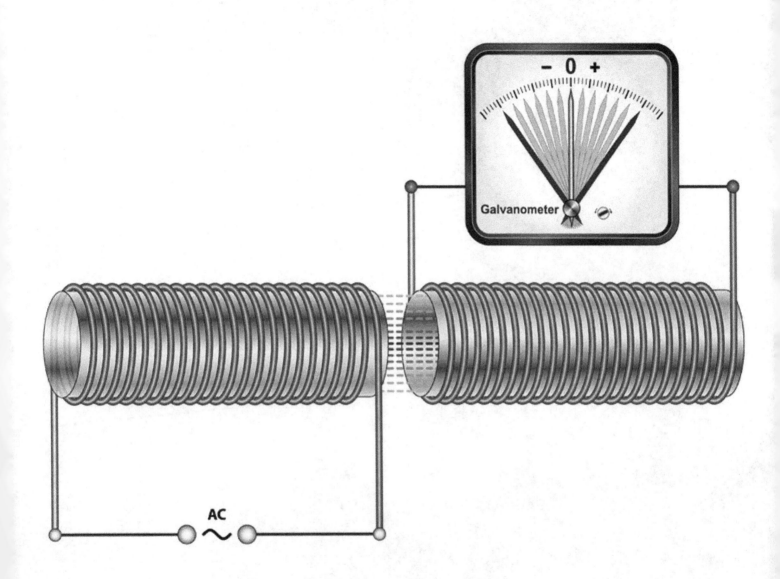

ELECTROMAGNETIC INDUCTION

If you have a magnetic field and you move a wire through it, the electrical current will begin to flow through that wire. One of the benefits of electromagnetism is that strong magnets can be shut off simply by stopping the electrical current. This differs from permanent magnets that always keep their magnetic force.

GENERATORS

Generators that create electricity take mechanical energy and movement and transform it using induction. A coil made of wire is spun at high speed between two magnets, one with a north pole and one with a south facing each other. A current of electricity is generated from this mechanical movement. The electricity generated can now be used to power devices.

ELECTRICAL POWER GENERATOR

The power needed to run a generator can come from many different types of sources. Two ways to power a generator with renewable energy are through wind power or solar power.

Remember electricity is powerful. Always make sure you have adult supervision when doing electrical experiments.

Awesome! Now you know more about electricity and magnetism. You can find more Physics books from Baby Professor by searching the website of your favorite book retailer.

CPSIA information can be obtained
at www.ICGtesting.com
Printed in the USA
LVHW061156280320
651489LV00033B/2912

9 781541 911499